21st Century Skills INNOVATION LIBRARY

EMERGING Tech

Self-Driving Cars

CHERRY LAKE PUBLISHING • ANN ARBOR, MICHIGAN

by Lauren Newman

A Note to Adults: Please review the instructions for the activities in this book before allowing children to do them. Be sure to help them with any activities you do not think they can safely complete on their own.

A Note to Kids: Be sure to ask an adult for help with these activities when you need it. Always put your safety first!

CHERRY LAKE Publishing

Published in the United States of America by Cherry Lake Publishing
Ann Arbor, Michigan
www.cherrylakepublishing.com

Content Editor: Matthew Lammi, PhD, Assistant Professor, College of Education, North Carolina State University, Raleigh, North Carolina
Reading Adviser: Marla Conn MS, Ed., Literacy specialist, Read-Ability, Inc.
Photo Credits: Cover and page 1, smoothgroover22 / tinyurl.com/jk5zywo / CC BY-SA 2.0; pages 4 and 29, ©Steve Lagreca/Shutterstock, Inc.; page 5, ©Looker_Studio/Shutterstock, Inc.; page 8, ©CLS Digital Arts/Shutterstock, Inc.; page 11, ©Chronicle/Alamy Stock Photo; page 12, ©ZUMA Press, Inc./Alamy Stock Photo; page 14, Steve Jurvetson / tinyurl.com/jrgwbzs / CC BY 2.0; pages 15 and 20, ©REUTERS/Alamy Stock Photo; pages 17, 18, and 19, ©dpa picture alliance/Alamy Stock Photo; page 23, ©All About Space/Shutterstock, Inc.; page 25, ©Narongsak Nagadhana/Shutterstock, Inc.; page 27, ©US State Department/Alamy Stock Photo

Library of Congress Cataloging-in-Publication Data has been filed and is available at catalog.loc.gov

Cherry Lake Publishing would like to acknowledge the work of the Partnership for 21st Century Learning. Please visit *www.p21.org* for more information.

Printed in the United States of America
Corporate Graphics

21st Century Skills INNOVATION LIBRARY

Contents

Chapter 1

No Driver Needed

Imagine zooming down the road in a car with no one driving. Everyone inside is relaxing and hanging out while the car does all the work. No, this isn't something from a science-fiction movie. It is the world of self-driving cars, a rapidly growing area of technology. A self-driving car is an automobile that can operate with little to no help from a human driver. It is also sometimes called a driverless car or **autonomous**

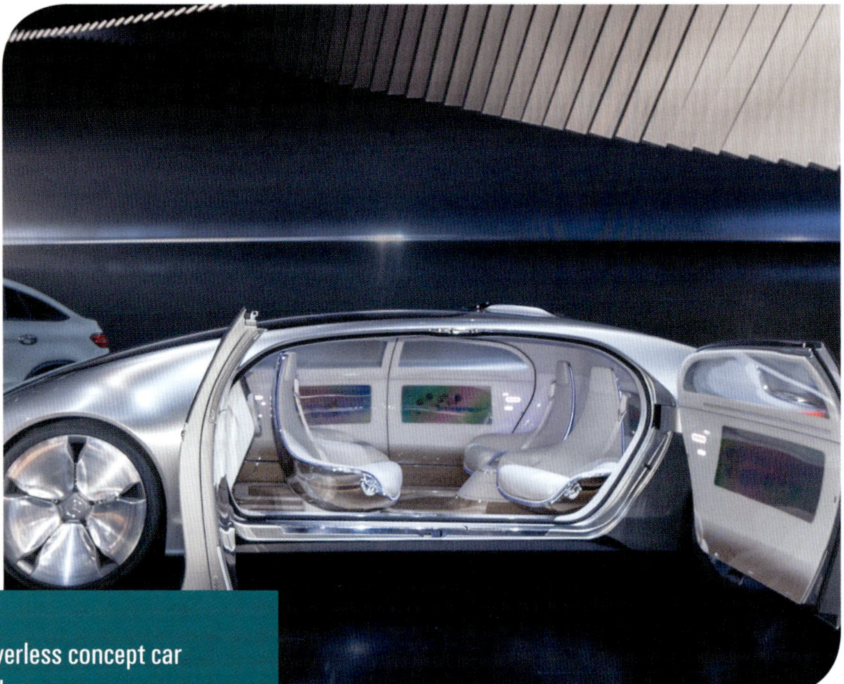

A Mercedes-Benz F 015 driverless concept car is displayed at a 2015 car show.

In most modern cars, drivers must manually control many of the vehicle's actions.

vehicle. Many experts predict that these incredible cars will be widely available to the public within the next few decades.

In fact, most cars available today are already partially autonomous. The National Highway Traffic Safety Administration organizes all automobiles into five different levels of autonomy. Level Zero describes cars that are completely driven by humans. The driver is responsible for all workings of the car, such as braking, steering, and gear-shifting. Only very old cars fall into this category.

Old Idea, New Technology

Believe it or not, the idea for self-driving cars is hundreds of years old. Around 1478, inventor and artist Leonardo da Vinci sketched an idea for a self-propelled cart that was able to move without being pushed. The cart measured 5.5 feet (1.7 meters) long and nearly 5 feet (1.5 m) wide. It worked by lifting a brake that released a coiled spring. This propelled the cart forward about 130 feet (39.6 m).

Da Vinci never actually built a model of his design. However, in 2004, engineers in Florence, Italy, built the driverless cart by following his instructions. They discovered that it worked just as da Vinci had planned.

All new cars in the United States are at least Level One vehicles. Level One involves some kind of **automation**. This can be something like electronic stability control (ESC). ESC helps prevent cars from skidding. It is required on all new cars in the United States. Antilock brake systems (ABS) are another common type of automated technology. ABS applies pressure to a car's brakes in a way that keeps the car from spinning out of control.

When at least two automated systems are combined, a car falls into the Level Two category. For example, some cars combine adaptive cruise control with lane centering technology. Adaptive cruise control helps a car adjust its speed to keep enough distance from the car in front of it. Lane centering helps keep the vehicle from shifting unexpectedly into other lanes. There are some Level Two automobiles on the road today. They tend to be high-end, luxury vehicles.

Level Three cars can mostly drive on their own. However, a human must be ready to take the wheel if necessary. The driver has the ability to **override** the automated operations and take control of steering, braking, or **accelerating**. There are a few Level Three cars being tested on the road today.

Level Four indicates a completely driverless car. A human sets the destination, and the vehicle performs all the driving functions for an entire trip. Vehicles at this level may not even have passengers. Imagine a car zipping around without anyone inside! These cars are being tested right now, but it will be awhile before the public is able to experience them.

Self-driving cars are equipped with **sensors**, computer programs, and other components. These help the car navigate roads and avoid obstacles. **Artificial intelligence** (AI) software imitates a human driver, allowing the car to make decisions about things like steering and braking.

Chapter 2

The Road to Autonomy

From electric motor starters to rearview cameras, automobile technology has steadily improved since cars were invented in the late 19th century. Every new advance attempts to make driving easier and more pleasurable for drivers and passengers.

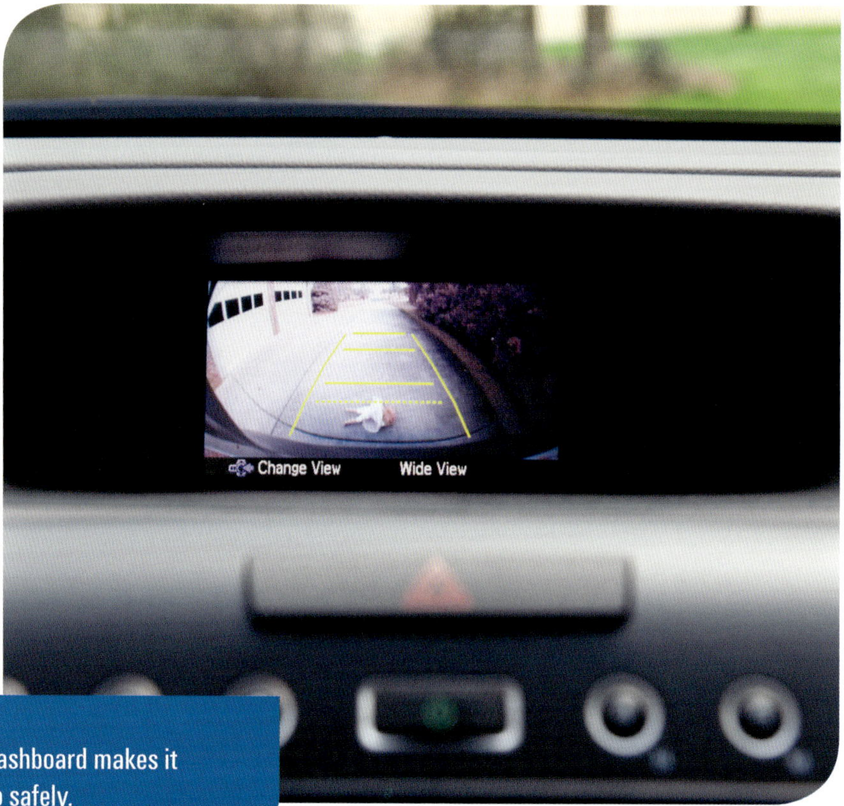

A rearview camera in the dashboard makes it easier for drivers to back up safely.

By the 1920s, automobiles were becoming common in big cities. Engineers began looking for ways to improve them. One such attempt came in 1925 with a driverless vehicle called the Linrrican Wonder.

The Linrrican Wonder was controlled by radio signals sent from another car following behind it. Using this method, it successfully traveled in busy New York City traffic. This was an amazing feat, but it was not practical to use two cars at a time. The idea for self-driving cars didn't end with the Linrrican Wonder, though. People continued to invent ways of automating vehicles.

At the 1939 World's Fair in New York, the General Motors (GM) car company sponsored an exhibit called Futurama. Designed by Norman Bel Geddes, the exhibit included a miniature model of an imagined future city. The model showed driverless cars speeding along the city's streets. In Bel Geddes's vision, these cars would be controlled using radio signals and powerful magnets underneath the roads.

GM tried to produce these kinds of driverless cars in real life but was not successful. The idea relied too heavily on making changes to existing roads. This was impractical and costly.

Slowly but Surely

In the 1970s, inventor Hans Moravec created the first robotic vehicle that was able to navigate around obstacles without human assistance. Based on an earlier invention called the Stanford Cart, Moravec's invention used a camera to send images of its environment to a computer. The computer used the images to tell the cart which way to go. This was an incredible breakthrough in technology. However, the device was extremely slow. Its computer took a long time to process the images and make a decision about which way to move. As a result, the cart could only travel 3.3 feet (1 m) every 10 to 15 minutes. It took the cart five hours to cross a single room!

In the following decades, computer technology advanced rapidly. Inventors began looking for ways to use this new technology in driverless cars. In the late 1980s, German engineer Ernst Dickmanns teamed up with the car company Mercedes-Benz to build a driverless van. Cameras and sensors on the van captured images of the road and the van's environment. Computers analyzed the data from the cameras and sensors. Then they used this information to control the van.

Nicknamed "VaMoRs," the van drove itself 12 miles (19.3 kilometers) at nearly 60 miles per hour (96.6 kph) down a real road. To prevent accidents, the road was closed to other traffic.

A drawing shows ideas for Norman Bel Geddes's Futurama exhibit at the 1939 World's Fair.

It wasn't until 1994 that Dickmanns was able to try his design in real traffic. Equipped with cameras, sensors, and computers, two driverless vehicles named Vita-2 and VaMP drove more than 620 miles (998 km) on a Paris highway at speeds of up to 81 miles per hour (130 kph).

A year later, Dickmanns's design was used to pilot a car from Munich, Germany, to Copenhagen, Denmark, and back. The trip was almost 1,000 miles (1,609 km)! The amazing feat showed that with the

Stanley waits to begin the 2005 DARPA Grand Challenge.

correct technology, a car could steer, accelerate, brake, change lanes, and pass other vehicles with little to no human action. Because of his innovations, Ernst Dickmanns is often referred to as the pioneer of the autonomous vehicle.

In 2004, the U.S. Defense Advanced Research Projects Agency (DARPA) created the Grand Challenge. This competition asked teams to build completely autonomous vehicles that could travel 142 miles (229 km) of California's Mojave Desert. Although no team completed the first Grand Challenge successfully, it encouraged more people to develop new and better technology.

In 2005, DARPA held a second challenge. This time there was a winner. The car was named Stanley, and it took 6 hours and 53 minutes to complete the course. Its average speed was about 20 miles per hour (32.2 kph). The captain of Stanley's team, Sebastian Thrun, would soon help revolutionize the self-driving car industry.

Chapter 3

Major Players

Today, Google is perhaps the most well-known company in the self-driving car industry. Google's founders, Larry Page and Sergey Brin, wanted to make driving safer. Page and Brin also thought about how self-driving cars could be more environmentally friendly than traditional cars. To help

One of Google's early self-driving cars completes an obstacle course.

Sebastian Thrun (left) celebrates after Stanley's victory at the 2005 DARPA Grand Challenge.

make this dream a reality, Google hired Sebastian Thrun and other leading engineers to begin working on self-driving cars.

Google started by equipping existing cars such as the Toyota Prius with sensors and software to turn them into self-driving vehicles. The engineers mounted LIDAR (light detection and ranging) equipment on each car's roof. LIDAR scans the area around the car to create a detailed 3-D map of the car's surrounding environment. Radar systems were

Finding the Way

A global positioning system (GPS) helps pinpoint the location of objects. GPS uses three parts: satellites, ground stations, and receivers. The 24 satellites orbit Earth from outer space. Ground stations use radar to track the satellites' positions. A receiver listens for the signals from the satellites and determines how far it is from them. If the receiver calculates its distance from four or more satellites, your exact position on Earth can be determined.

GPS was originally designed for use by the military. However, now anyone with a smartphone or other mobile GPS device can receive the signals sent by the satellites. It plays an important role in all of the latest self-driving cars.

installed in the front and rear bumpers. These are used to calculate the distances to obstacles such as other cars on the road. Tire sensors were added to help the car detect sideways movement. A computer in the trunk uses AI software to connect to all the sensors and imitate human decision making. This software also controls actions such as steering and braking. Google engineers also added an override function so a human driver could take control of the car at any time.

Google tested its vehicles for years all over the state of California and had much success. The

Google's latest cars have a round, modern look.

cars' destinations had to be programmed by a human. Other than that, they functioned completely autonomously. Google's self-driving cars proved that they can slow down or accelerate, obey traffic signals, change lanes, avoid obstacles, and even pass other traffic, all while maintaining a speed of 25 miles per hour (40 kph).

In 2014, Google decided to take the next step and build its own driverless cars from scratch. The company's engineers designed a small, electric self-driving car. The car does not include a steering wheel or gas and brake pedals. Instead, there are two main control buttons. One starts the car, and the other shuts the car down in case of an emergency. These cars do not even require a human to sit inside!

Google is not the only company to try its hand at driverless car technology. Some other car companies that are developing driverless cars include General Motors, Audi, Tesla, and Mercedes-Benz. These

The interior of a recent Google car looks very different from most traditional vehicles.

The Audi A7 contains several self-driving features.

companies have been adding self-driving technology to their existing cars with much success.

Self-parking is one automated feature that many car manufacturers have equipped their cars with. In 2013, Audi's A7 model became the first car to park itself without any human help.

In 2014 Audi made further advances when it introduced its traffic jam assistant. Using a combination of sensors, cameras, LIDAR, and a computer, the assistant can take over the controls of the vehicle during traffic jams. It only works at speeds under 40 miles per hour (64 kph). Even though the car is driving itself, its human driver must remain alert and active at all times. In fact, cameras pointing at the driver can detect whether or not the driver's eyes are open or closed.

Tesla jumped into the self-driving car game in October 2015 with the autopilot feature for its S and

A driver uses the autopilot feature of a Tesla Model S.

X model vehicles. As with Audi's traffic jam assistant, drivers still need to be alert at all times. The car takes over driving when conditions permit, but only after the driver tells it to. The driver is still very much in control of the car and can decide when to turn autopilot on or off.

GM started testing cars equipped with self-driving technology in May 2016. GM calls its technology Super Cruise. Other companies' autonomous systems require the driver to keep a hand on the steering wheel to show that the driver is still alert. GM's system is different—it allows the driver to take his or her hands off the wheel for extended periods of time. GM also announced plans to one day bring its driverless car technology to the popular ride-sharing service Lyft. This could someday result in a fleet of self-driving taxis.

Right now, consumers cannot purchase fully driverless cars. However, these companies are all seeking to change that in the future. All of the companies involved in creating and testing self-driving cars are competing with each other. Each wants to be the first to bring the technology to the general public.

Chapter 4

Benefits and Concerns

Safety is perhaps both the main benefit and main concern noted about self-driving cars. While many people believe self-driving cars will make the roads safer, others believe that having a computer in control of a car will bring problems.

In 2015, car accidents caused more than 38,000 deaths in the United States alone. More than 4 million other people suffered injuries serious enough to require a hospital visit. In most of these cases, the accidents were caused by human error. Many experts believe that self-driving cars have the ability to lower those numbers. Computers don't get distracted by text messages, alcohol, impatience, or exhaustion—all of which cause accidents. Some experts believe that self-driving cars could reduce deaths from car accidents by about 90 percent.

Self-driving cars may use less gasoline because they will drive more **efficiently**. This will reduce traffic jams on the roads and lessen the amount of

Driverless cars could have a major effect on reducing traffic jams.

pollution from cars. Driverless cars may also lead to more people sharing cars. This could further reduce the number of cars on the road and the pollution created. The more self-driving cars are on the road, the more they will be able to communicate with each other. Sensors in the cars will enable them to drive closer together. This will increase highway capacity and reduce traffic jams.

Self-driving cars will also be a big help to people who are not able to drive. Right now, people who are blind or have other conditions that do not allow

Hacking on the Highway

In 2013, automotive cybersecurity researchers Charlie Miller and Chris Valasek were able to take over the controls of a Toyota Prius by hacking into its computer systems. They were remotely able to do things like slam on the brakes and honk the car's horn.

In 2016, Miller and Valasek hacked another car. This time it was a Jeep Cherokee. They were able to do even more serious things this time, including jerking the wheel to the side while the car traveled at high speeds. This showed that self-driving cars are still very vulnerable to attacks from hackers. They will need to have strong security systems to keep drivers and passengers safe.

them to drive must rely on others for transportation. Imagine if these people could now go anywhere thanks to a self-driving car.

Driverless cars have many potential benefits, but the technology is not perfect. Computers can stop working or be affected by viruses. They can also be **hacked**. This has led many people to distrust the idea of driverless cars. In addition, many people do not like the idea that GPS, radar, and various other systems in a driverless car can be easily tracked. They believe it could lead to an invasion of privacy.

Self-driving cars rely on cameras and other sensors to function. But what if the cameras cannot detect

Many people are worried that self-driving cars might not be able to react as quickly as human drivers in difficult weather conditions.

the lines of the road due to a snowstorm or heavy rain? What if the driverless car is faced with having to hit one obstacle to avoid hitting another? What decision will it make? While the computer has been "taught" to think like a human, it isn't a human.

Google's self-driving car was involved in its first crash in February 2016. In order to avoid hitting a pile of sandbags that were near a storm drain, the car veered into a passing bus. The accident was minor.

However, it showed that the computer doesn't always make the best choice when faced with a split-second decision. In some situations, there isn't even a good choice to make. How will the car decide what to do when none of its choices produce a safe outcome? These are questions that cannot yet be answered. Manufacturers of self-driving cars are constantly working to improve the safety and AI of their vehicles, but the technology is still far from perfect.

Another concern about self-driving cars is the cost. Equipping cars with LIDAR, radar, cameras, GPS, computers, and other equipment can cost thousands of dollars. In 2014, a Toyota Prius self-driving car was said to cost around $320,000. This is far more than the average consumer can afford to spend on a car.

The price of self-driving vehicles is expected to drop over the next several decades as the technology improves and becomes more common. By the year 2035, it is estimated that the cost of adding the necessary technology to a self-driving car will only be about $3,000. For now, though, the average person would probably not be able to afford a self-driving car.

Chapter 5

The Future of Driverless Cars

Many people believe that our future will include self-driving cars for everyone. Others believe this dream is a long way off, if it ever happens at all. However, it is safe to say that some form of self-driving cars will be a part of our future. Companies are pouring millions of dollars into driverless cars. The U.S. government is even creating new laws for these cars, proving that it thinks driverless cars are

Then U.S. Secretary of State John Kerry inspects a Google self-driving car in 2016.

Paving the Way

The city of Pittsburgh, Pennsylvania, announced in September 2016 that it will allow the ride-sharing service Uber to operate self-driving cars within the city. It is unclear how autonomous these Uber cars will be. However, they will have at least some self-driving components. This will make Pittsburgh the first U.S. city to allow commuters to ride in self-driving cars. If the experiment is successful, more cities will undoubtedly hop on board.

here to stay. Several states have passed laws allowing self-driving cars to be tested on their roads. However, some states require a human driver to be behind the wheel of a self-driving car at all times. This would make Google's driverless car illegal, because it doesn't even have a wheel! Some states already have laws requiring drivers to keep one hand on the steering wheel at all times. How do GM's Super Cruise cars factor into this? That's a tricky question.

Furthermore, no one knows how car insurance will work with self-driving cars. Can a person be held responsible for an accident caused by a driverless car? These are questions that will need to be answered in the future.

It's even possible that in the future, people won't own their own self-driving cars. Instead, they will use apps to summon self-driving cars as needed from a

Are you ready to take a ride in the cars of the future?

fleet of waiting vehicles. These cars could eliminate parking problems all over big cities. Instead of driving to work and parking all day in a garage, drivers may be able to request a self-driving car to pick them up and drop them off. When not in use, the car could just drive away to be used by someone else.

Cars have been evolving for decades. Although the idea for self-driving cars is not brand new, it has become more practical than ever before. Imagine zooming down the road, lying back with your feet up and a book open in your lap. This is not yet a reality, but who knows what the future will bring? Will self-driving cars become a safe and trusted part of everyday life? Only time will tell.

Glossary

accelerating (ak-SEL-ur-ay-ting) changing speed

artificial intelligence (ahr-tuh-FISH-uhl in-TEL-ih-juhns) the science of making computers do things that previously needed human intelligence

automation (aw-tuh-MAY-shuhn) the use of machines rather than people to do jobs

autonomous (aw-TAH-nuh-muhs) able to function without any assistance

efficiently (ih-FISH-uhnt-lee) without wasting time or energy

hacked (HAKD) accessed or took control of a computer system remotely and without permission

override (oh-vur-RIDE) to take manual control over an automated system

sensors (SEN-surz) instruments that can detect and measure changes and transmit the information to a controlling device

Find Out More

BOOKS

Marsico, Katie. *Self-Driving Cars.* New York: Children's Press, 2016.

Watson, Stephanie. *What Is the Future of Self-Driving Cars?* San Diego: ReferencePoint Press, 2017.

WEB SITES

Encyclopedia Britannica: The Emergence of Driverless Cars

www.britannica.com/topic/Emergence-of-Driverless-Cars-The-2045163

Find out how driverless cars have come closer to reality in recent years.

Waymo

https://waymo.com/

Learn more about Google's efforts to build self-driving cars for everyday use.

Index

About the Author

Lauren Newman is a school library, media, and technology specialist in Columbus, New Jersey. She loves to read and travel, and she is excited to one day ride in a self-driving car. This is her second book.